Sky High

CONTENTS

NATIONAL GEOGRAPHIC   Hampton-Brown

School Publishing

Words with <u>ie</u>, <u>igh</u>

Look at each picture. Read the words.

_ie
_igh

Example:

p<u>ie</u>

n<u>igh</u>t

fl<u>ie</u>s

l<u>igh</u>t

t<u>ie</u>

h<u>igh</u>way

2

High Frequency Words
above
again
away
change
seven
sometimes

Key Words

Look at the picture.
Read the sentences.

Sunset

1. The sun is **above**, far **away** in the sky.

2. It is **seven** o'clock.

3. See the sky **change** as the sun sets.

4. **Sometimes** the sky turns red.

5. The sun will rise **again** the next day.

Where is the sun?
How does the sky change?

Day Sky and Night Sky

by Maya Martinez

The sun rises. It is daytime. Look up.

What is in the day sky?

sun

You might see the
sun. If the sun is shining,
the sky will be bright. Bright
sun can mean a hot day.

high clouds

low clouds

You might see clouds. Have you seen clouds high in the sky? High clouds look thin and white. Low clouds look fat and fluffy.

clouds

Sometimes gray clouds fill the sky.
This means rain might come.

Clouds can hide the sun. The sun is still
in the sky. It is above the clouds.

The sun sets. Daylight gets less bright.
Nighttime comes. Soon it is not hot.
It is mild.

The night sky is not the same as the day sky. Look up. What is in the night sky?

phases of the moon

full moon

You might see the moon. The moon will change each night.

When the moon is full, it has a shape like a pie. It shines with a bright light. Sometimes you see just a bit of it.

You might see stars. Stars are big, but they are far away. That is why they seem so small.

The moon sets. The sun rises. Day is on the way. Day and night change places again and again. ❖

Words with <u>ie</u>, <u>igh</u>

Read these words.

night	day	light	bright
child	might	dark	boy

Find the words with
the long **i** sound.
Use letters to build them.

n   i   g   h   t

Choose words from the box
to tell your partner about the sky.

The _day_ sky is
bright.

1.    **2.**

Syllables

Look at each picture. Read the words.

Example:

rainbow
▲

kitten
▲

window
▲

rabbit
▲

yellow mittens
▲   ▲

button
▲

High Frequency
Words

above

again

away

change

seven

sometimes

Key Words

Read the clues.

Answer the riddle.

What Is It?

1. It is far **away**, high **above** in the sky.

2. It has **seven** colors.

3. **Sometimes** it can **change** from one to two.

4. Take a look **again**.

What seven colors do you see?

Phonics Games

NGReach.com

15

Rainbows
by Rowan Obach

What is a rainbow?

A rainbow is a band of colors. Follow the band with your eyes.

The band stretches from one side
of the sky to the other. Its ends seem
to be hidden.

How many colors are in a rainbow?

A rainbow has seven colors. Why?
Light helps make a rainbow. Light has
seven colors.

Can you name the
colors in light?

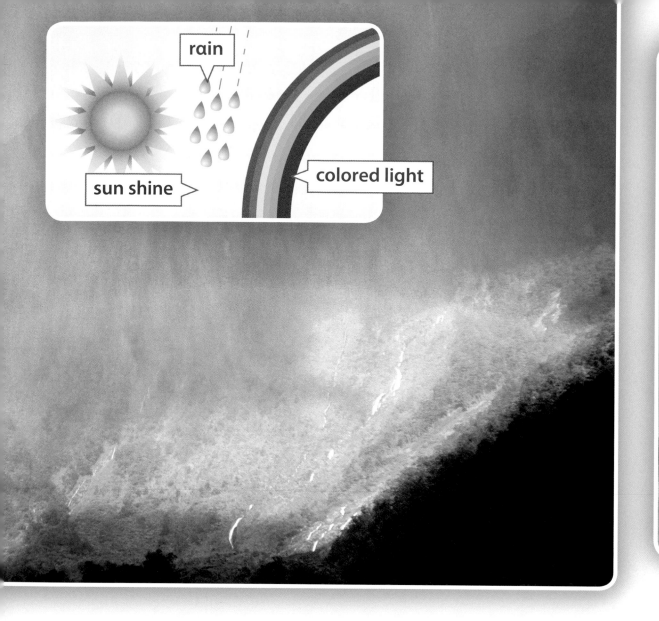

rain

sun shine

colored light

What makes a rainbow?

It rains. Then it gets sunny. The sun shines through the rain droplets.

Look at the sky away from the sun. A rainbow shows up. Red is on the outside. Violet is on the inside. You can see green and yellow in the rainbow, too.

Sometimes two rainbows show up. One rainbow is above the other. You may not see that again.

waterfall

Where are rainbows?

Check the sky when it rains. Spray a hose into the air. Look at waves in the sea. Watch a waterfall. Rainbows may show up in these places.

23

Not everyone will be lucky and see a rainbow when it rains. If you see a rainbow outside your window, you can feel happy. ❖

Syllables

Read these words.

yellow	wet	sun	huge
insect	rainbow	droplet	pillow

Find the words with two syllables. Use letters to build them.

y e l l o w

Talk Together

Choose words from the box to tell your partner about the weather.

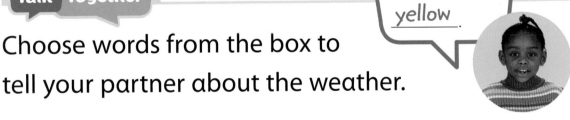

The _sun_ is _yellow_.

1.

2.

3.

Riddle Time

Look at the picture with a partner. Take turns reading the riddles. Then say and point to the answers.

1. This bright object in the sky rises again and again.

2. These two animals fly high above in the sky.

kite

crickets

rabbit

26

crows

sun

③ This object flies on a string sometimes.

④ This object is hidden away in a basket.

⑤ These seven are looking for pie.

basket

napkin

insects

pie

Acknowledgments
Grateful acknowledgment is given to the authors, artists, photographers, museums, publishers, and agents for permission to reprint copyrighted material. Every effort has been made to secure the appropriate permission. If any omissions have been made or if corrections are required, please contact the Publisher.

Photographic Credits
CVR (Cover) Vladimir Piskunov/iStockphoto. **2** (br) PhotoDisc/Getty Images. (cl) Floortje/ iStockphoto. (cl) Julie de Leseleuc/iStockphoto. (cr) koksharov dmitry/iStockphoto. (tl) Artville. (tr) SeaHorse/Shutterstock. **3** (b) Liz Garza Williams/Hampton-Brown/National Geographic School Publishing. (t) DigitalStock/Corbis. **4-5** (bg) Iakov Kalinin/Shutterstock. **5** (r) Sorin Popa/Shutterstock. **6** (b) PhotoDisc/Getty Images. (t) Norbert Rosing/National Geographic Image Collection. **7** Laurie Knight/iStockphoto. **8** Nadiya/Shutterstock. **9** (b) Leigh Schindler/ iStockphoto. (t) Soubrette/iStockphoto. **10** (b) Soubrette/iStockphoto. (t) David Scheuber/ Shutterstock. **10-11** (bg) Ian McKinnell/Getty Images. **12** DigitalStock/Corbis. **13** (bl) PhotoDisc/Getty Images. (br) amana images inc./Alamy Images. (t) Liz Garza Williams/ Hampton-Brown/National Geographic School Publishing. **14** (bl) Siede Preis/Photodisc/Alamy Images. (br) Ingram Publishing/Superstock. (cl) travis manley/Shutterstock. (cr) Radius Images/ Alamy Images. (tl) Eyewire. (tr) Digital Stock/Corbis. **15** (b) Liz Garza Williams/Hampton-Brown/ National Geographic School Publishing. (t) Karl Weatherly/Corbis. **16-17** Pichugin Dmitry/ Shutterstock. **18** Julian Barkway/iStockphoto. **19** (b) Alfred Pasieka/Peter Arnold, Inc.. (t) Image Source/Corbis. **20** Onne van der Wal/Corbis. **21** Gelpi/Shutterstock. **22** Kurt Stier/ Corbis/Jupiterimages. **23** Maciej Korzekwa/iStockphoto. **24** (bbg) Alvaro Arroyo/iStockphoto. (bg) Helen King/Corbis. (fg) Jesus Jauregui/iStockphoto. **25** (bc) Graham Prentice/ Shutterstock. (bl) Eyewire. (br) Viktor Penner/iStockphoto. (t) Liz Garza Williams/Hampton-Brown/National Geographic School Publishing. (t) Liz Garza Williams/Hampton-Brown/National Geographic School Publishing.

Illustrator Credits
26-27 Sharon Tancredi

The National Geographic Society
John M. Fahey, Jr., President & Chief Executive Officer
Gilbert M. Grosvenor, Chairman of the Board

National Geographic School Publishing
Hampton-Brown
www.NGSP.com

Printed in the USA.
RR Donnelley, Jefferson City, MO

ISBN: 978-0-7362-8043-3

12 13 14 15 16 17 18 19
10 9 8 7 6 5 4

New High Frequency Words

- above
- again
- away
- change
- seven
- sometimes

Target Sound/Spellings

Words with <u>ie</u>, <u>igh</u>	Syllables
Selection: **Day Sky and Night Sky** bright daylight high light might night nighttime pie	**Selection:** **Rainbows** droplet follow happy hidden inside lucky rainbow(s) sunny window yellow